TABLE OF CONTENTS

For the Teacher

This reproducible study guide consists of instructional material to use in conjunction with the novel *The Book Thief*. Written in chapter-by-chapter format, the guide contains a synopsis, pre-reading activities, vocabulary and comprehension exercises, as well as extension activities to be used as follow-up to the novel.

NOVEL-TIES are either for whole class instruction using a single title or for group instruction where each group uses a different novel appropriate to its reading level. Depending upon the amount of time allotted to it in the classroom, each novel, with its guide and accompanying lessons, may be completed in two to four weeks.

The first step in using NOVEL-TIES is to distribute to each student a copy of the novel and a folder containing all of the duplicated worksheets. Begin instruction by selecting several pre-reading activities in order to set the stage for the reading ahead. Vocabulary exercises for each chapter always precede the reading so that new words will be reinforced in the context of the book. Use the questions on the chapter worksheets for class discussion or as written exercises.

The benefits of using NOVEL-TIES are numerous. Students read good literature in the original, rather than in abridged or edited form. The good reading habits formed by practice in focusing on interpretive comprehension and literary techniques will be transferred to the books students read independently. Passive readers become active, avid readers.

SYNOPSIS

This is the story of Liesel Meminger, a young German girl who is placed in foster care during the early years of World War II by a mother too ill to care for her any longer. On the train to Molching, a small German town where she and her brother are to stay for the duration of the war, Liesel's brother dies from tuberculosis. On this terrible day, Liesel discovers a copy of *The Gravedigger's Handbook*, the first of a series of books she will find or steal. "Death," the personification who narrates the book, will always think of Liesel as the book thief; curious about this lonely, intelligent child, he decides to tell her story.

Liesel is left on her own to adapt to her new life with the Hubermanns, a middle-aged couple with two grown children, one a card-carrying Nazi soldier. Rosa Hubermann, the foster mother, is a choleric, short-tempered woman with hidden reservoirs of sympathy. Hans Hubermann, in contrast, is a gentle house-painter who plays the accordion and wants only a life of harmony. It is Hans who makes Liesel feel at home and tends to her through the long months of nightmares in the wake of her abandonment.

These are tumultuous years, as Hitler's policies ravage the Jewish communities and bring privation and suffering to Europe. Even Death is appalled by the numbers of souls he must carry off. There are serious food shortages, book burnings, and the assignment of air raid shelters. Liesel goes to school, making fast friends with Rudy Steiner, her irrepressible neighbor and classmate, while Rosa Hubermann takes in laundry to supplement the family income. Work is scarce for Hans; he is not a member of the Nazi Party, having violated the Aryan code by painting over the hateful graffiti on the door of a Jewish shop. His lack of steady employment, however, gives Hans time to teach Liesel to read, and she slowly becomes a lover of words.

These are hungry years, as Rosa loses many of her customers and feeds the family on watery soup and bread. Rudy and Liesel join a local gang to steal food. Liesel, though, would rather steal books, and finds in the unprotected library of the mayor's home a treasure trove of volumes. An odd, secretive relationship develops between the grieving wife of the mayor and the book thief. Life takes on a pattern of surface conformity and covert acts of petty crime and resistance. Rudy and Liesel despise Nazi brutality, but join the Hitler youth groups that have sprung up all over Germany.

When a young Jewish refugee comes to hide out in the basement of the Hubermanns' home, the inhumanity of Nazism takes on a human face. Max Vandenburg is the son of a man who saved Hans Hubermann's life during the first World War. Hans owes his dead friend the act of compassion that could easily jeopardize the lives of every-one in his household.

During his months in the basement, Max becomes part of the family and forges a strong bond with Liesel. But when another act of compassion on the part of Hans makes Max's continued residence with the Hubermanns too risky, the young Jewish man must flee. Liesel encounters him later in the war, when he has become a prisoner at Dachau concentration camp. Yet, Death will not come to carry Max's soul away yet. It is the Hubermanns who will die in an air strike that decimates the neighborhood and leaves Liesel alone again. In the midst of her loss and despair, the mayor's wife comes to claim her and give her another home.

In 1945, the war has ended. Liesel is helping out in Alex Steiner's tailor shop when Max Vandenburg reappears, having miraculously survived Dachau. The story jumps forward in time, and Liesel is now an old woman living in Sydney, Australia. Death has read her story and gently comes to claim her soul. He will not soon forget the touching history of the book thief, one of the good Germans who steadfastly kept her humanity and her courage during one of the most terrible eras of modern history.

BACKGROUND INFORMATION

The Seeds of World War II

During the 1930s, Germany, soundly defeated in World War I, gathered strength under the leadership of the fanatical nationalist Adolf Hitler. Hitler and his Nazi Party rearmed Germany, breaking the Versailles Treaty of 1919 that had been designed to keep peace throughout Europe. Hitler's trained thugs murdered political opponents, clearing his way to power. The Nazi leader entered into a series of negotiations that would allow Germany to dominate eastern Europe. Envisioning themselves as a superior or "master" race, the Nazis ultimately planned to rule northern Europe as well.

Hitler carefully laid his political groundwork. The 1934 non-aggression pact he signed with Poland was a ploy to keep the Poles from arming against Germany. Hitler then signed an agreement with Stalin, Russia's leader, dividing Poland between them. In 1936, the Italian leader Mussolini also signed a non-aggression pact with Germany. In 1938, the Nazi-run government incorporated Austria and parts of Czechoslovakia into an empire known as "the Third Reich."

The stage was set for another world war. When France and Great Britain failed to act quickly to stop Hitler, the Germans opened hostilities, launching a massive air offensive on Warsaw and the surrounding area. The Nazis gained control of Poland within three weeks. With Poland as its base, the German army launched its campaign across Europe, leaving destruction and death in its wake.

Hitler and the Jews

In 1933, when Adolf Hitler became Chancellor of Germany, a national census showed that the Jewish population of Germany numbered around 600,000, representing less than one percent of the country's total population. Of these, approximately eighty percent held German citizenship. The remaining twenty percent were mainly Jews of Polish descent. Why did this ethnic group pose such a serious threat to Hitler's ideal Germany? The answer lies in the long history of anti-Semitism, particularly in Europe. Jews were persecuted in Spain and in Russia, where they were coerced to convert to Christianity or face dire consequences. In general, the Jews tended to retain their own religious and cultural beliefs, although some did convert in order to conform to social expectations. Kept out of many professions, Jews sometimes acted as money-lenders and were then scapegoated for the economic problems of the citizenry.

Hitler was not Germany's first rabid anti-Semite. He was greatly influenced by Karl Lueger, mayor of Vienna, Austria from 1897 to 1910. The leader of the Christian Social Party, Lueger garnered voters with his platform of religious and racial homogeneity. He drew his support largely from the lower middle class, exploiting prejudices and attributing financial hardships to the practices of the Jews.

Hitler found it politically expedient to take the same approach. In *Mein Kampf*, he accused Jews of deliberately attempting to pollute the pure German gene pool, of robbing Aryans, and of destroying the nation's social fabric. His propaganda became effective during the Great Depression, when the economic collapse put many out of work. Hitler's government introduced a strict program of segregation of the Jews, prohibiting them from attending mainstream schools and from doing business with Aryans, or "pure" Germans. The government smiled on thugs who destroyed Jewish property and terrorized Jewish communities.

With the passing of the Nuremberg Laws of 1935, German Jews lost their rights as citizens, and intermarriage between Jews and non-Jews was prohibited. As acts of violence and outrage against Jews increased, many fled Germany. Those who remained behind suffered greatly from lack of food and medicines. Organized death squads killed thousands in Germany and Eastern Europe. In 1938, the assassination of a German diplomat by a Jewish teenager touched off a Nazi retaliation of astonishing brutality—*Kristallnacht*, or "night of broken glass," when Nazis and SS storm troopers smashed the windows in Jewish stores, committing murder and acts of violence along the way. There were also mass arrests that resulted in the expropriation of Jewish monies and properties by government officials.

In 1942, the Nazis instituted the concentration camps, where prisoners were worked to death, shot, or gassed. The vast majority of German and Polish Jews ended up in these camps; relatively few survived Hitler's Final Solution. The Allies liberated the camps in 1945, with the defeat of the Axis Powers. Hitler would not live to face trial for the genocide he had orchestrated. He committed suicide in April, 1945, when the Red Army invaded Germany.

Jesse Owens

James Cleveland Owens was born in Lawrence County, Alabama in 1913 and raised in Cleveland, Ohio. Owens, the grandson of a slave, was often sick as a child. He was given the name *Jesse* by a teacher in Cleveland who did not understand his country accent.

Jesse grew up in poverty, taking odd jobs delivering groceries, loading freight cars, and working in a shoe repair shop as a young teenager. During this time, he realized that he had a passion for running, encouraged by his junior-high track coach.

Owens first came to national attention when he was a high school student and equaled the record of 9.4 seconds in the 100-yard dash and long-jumped 24 feet 9½ inches at the 1933 National High School Championship of Chicago.

Owens attended Ohio State University where he won a record of eight individual NCAA championships. Although Owens enjoyed athletic success, he had to live off-campus with other African-American athletes. When he traveled with the team, he had to eat at "black-only" restaurants, and sleep in "black-only" hotels.

In 1936 Owens was selected to compete for the United States in the Summer Olympics in Berlin. Adolf Hitler was using the games to show the world a resurgent Nazi Germany and the superiority of the Aryan race. Owens, however, won four gold medals. Hitler publicly snubbed Owens, shaking hands only with German victors.

When Owens returned to the United States, he was given a hero's welcome, but it was short-lived. As an African-American before the Civil Rights movement in America, Owens suffered the injustices of his race and eventually filed for bankruptcy. It wasn't until 1966 that his rehabilitation began and he lived out the rest of his life as a U.S. goodwill ambassador. Owens died of lung cancer at the age of 66.

PRE-READING ACTIVITIES AND DISCUSSION QUESTIONS

1. Preview the book by reading the title and the author's name and by looking at the illustration on the cover. What do you think this novel will be about? When and where does it take place? Have you read any other books by the same author?

2. **Social Studies Connection:** The Holocaust killed six million Jews and millions of other "undesirable" Europeans, including Gypsies, political dissenters, disabled people, and Soviet prisoners of war. Read the Background Information on page three of this study guide and do some additional research to learn more about the genocide orchestrated by Hitler and his Nazi troops and how it affected European Jewry and other minorities. Record information in the first two columns of the K-W-L chart, such as the one below. Fill in the third column after you finish the book.

What I Know −K−	What I Would Like To Know −W−	What I Learned −L−

3. Have you read any other books or seen any films about the Holocaust and the rise of the Nazis to power? How did these circumstances affect the lives of the characters in the book or film? What did you learn about life for both Jews and non-Jews during World War II?

4. A stereotype is an oversimplified image of a group of people, usually held in common by some part of society. How can stereotypes be harmful? What do you think people can do to overcome stereotyping? Have you noticed any examples of stereotyping in your community or in the media?

5. The narrator of *The Book Thief* is Death, who is not portrayed in the usual way. As you read the book, consider how Death is characterized and determine how he differs from the usual portrayal in literature and art.

6. *The Book Thief* urges the reader to consider the power of words—both the written and spoken word. As you read, think about the ways the characters in the story were affected by words and how they influenced others through language. Then think about the significance of words in your own life.

7. Read the Background Information on Jesse Owens on page five of this study guide and do some additional research to learn why Rudy, one of the main characters in the book, idolized this track star.

Pre-Reading Activities and Discussion Questions (cont.)

8. In wartime, conventional notions of morality and legality are continually tested. Throughout *The Book Thief*, the main characters must make decisions about how to behave, decisions that usually prove fateful. How do you think you would act if the law dictated that you treat others unfairly? Do you think you would follow the law or obey the call of your own conscience?

9. In this novel, characters are sometimes pushed to the limits of their courage, endurance, and resourcefulness. In *The Book Thief*, wartime conditions lead characters to lie, steal, hide, and pretend loyalties that they do not actually feel. With a group of classmates, discuss possible situations that might test a person's survival skills, such as cunning, speed, powers of observation, and the ability to adapt to stressful circumstances. Make a list of these situations. Which ones seem most challenging?

10. This novel explores nontraditional, or unusual, relationships. Characters are brought together by hardship and chance, gradually developing strong bonds of attachment. What kinds of family relationships have you heard of or experienced, other than those created by blood ties? Make a list of those relationships and reflect on them as you read *The Book Thief*.

PROLOGUE, PART 1

Vocabulary: Draw a line from each word on the left to its definition on the right. Then use the numbered words to fill in the blanks in the sentences below.

1.	affable	a.	showing intensity of feeling
2.	lethal	b.	promising; favorable
3.	vehement	c.	harsh; grating; disorderly
4.	auspicious	d.	scold
5.	raucous	e.	state of disease, death, or unwholesomeness
6.	catalyst	f.	fatal; deadly
7.	abducted	g.	without warmth of feeling
8.	morbidity	h.	carried off unlawfully
9.	berate	i.	agent that stirs a person or thing to action
10.	frigid	j.	easy to approach; pleasant

. . . .

1. After working as the congresswoman's aide, I was a(n) _____ supporter of her candidacy for governor.

2. Most people consider a wedding to be a(n) _____ occasion.

3. The _____ of the movie makes it unsuitable for children to view.

4. Uncontrolled by their government or military officers, ordinary soldiers _____ enemy foot soldiers and officers.

5. Thrusting out her hand stiffly, my new neighbor offered me a(n) _____ but polite welcome.

6. This _____ flock of crows frightened away all of the smaller birds in the area.

7. The bite of a scorpion is not always _____, but it is certainly painful.

8. I waited for my teacher to _____ me when I failed to turn in my report on time.

9. A persuasive leader can be a(n) _____ for positive or negative change.

10. My uncle's _____ manner makes him a favorite with children and adults.

Prologue, Part 1 (cont.)

Questions:

1. What did Death find painful about his duties?
2. What mistake did Death make at the train line?
3. What tragedy struck Liesel's family while aboard the train?
4. Why were Liesel and her brother Werner supposed to be placed in foster care in January 1939?
5. Why did Death think it was foolish for the poor to travel to escape poverty?
6. Why was the book about grave digging significant to Liesel?
7. What helped Liesel adjust to her foster home?
8. Why was school a failure for Liesel?
9. What was Rudy's father trying to teach his son on the night of the Jesse Owens incident?
10. Why did Liesel insist on participating in the reading examination? Why did it end in disaster?
11. Why did the narrator's workload increase in the beginning of September 1939?

Questions for Discussion:

1. Why do you suppose that Death saw life in terms of color and referred to color in terms of taste? What tastes would you assign to colors such as red, blue, green, yellow, and purple?
2. Why do you think the Hubermanns insisted that Liesel call them "Mama" and "Papa"?
3. Do you think German citizens, such as Alex Steiner or Hans Hubermann, were justified in showing passive acceptance to the Nazi regime? What else might they have done?
4. Do you think Liesel's hostility toward Ludwig Schmeikl was justified? In your opinion, what was the primary cause of her attack?

Literary Devices:

I. *Point of View*—Point of view in literature refers to the person telling the story. This person is called the narrator. The story may be told by the author (first-person narrative) or by a character in the story (third-person narrative). From what point of view is this story told?

_____

_____

Why do you think the author chose this point of view? Is the narrator objective or opinionated? Are the narrator's frequent comments thought-provoking or intrusive?

_____

_____

Prologue, Part 1 (cont.)

II. *Personification*—Personification is a device in which an author grants human qualities to nonhuman objects or concepts. For example, in this novel, death is personified
and given the attributes of thoughts and emotions. For example,

> I buckled—I became interested. In the girl. Curiosity got the
> better of me, and I resigned myself to stay as long as my schedule
> allowed, and I watched.

How does the use of personification shape the reader's reactions to Death? What is
surprising or unexpected about the author's personification of this universal condition?

_____

_____

_____

III. *Metaphor*—A metaphor is a suggested or implied comparison between two unlike
objects. For example:

> On the footpath, Liesel stood with her papa and Rudy. Hans
> Hubermann wore a face with the shades pulled down.

What is being compared?

_____

What does this reveal about Hans Hubermann's reaction to the Nazi rally?

_____

_____

IV. *Irony*—Irony refers to the difference between the way things seem to be and the way
things are. What was ironic about the first book that Liesel "stole"?

_____

_____

_____

Prologue, Part 1 (cont.)

Literary Elements:

I. *Setting*—Setting refers to the time and place where the events of a novel occur. What is the setting of *The Book Thief*?

_____

How does the setting shape the events in the novel?

_____

_____

II. *Characterization*—Compare the characters of Liesel and Rudy in the Venn diagram below. Record the ways they are alike in the overlapping part of the circles. Add information as you continue to read the book.

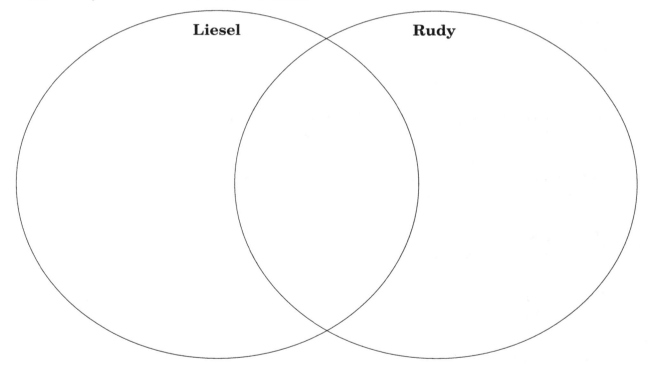

Writing Activity:

Write about a real or imagined day in your life in which you use color imagery to describe the setting and the events that happen, as the author did in the Prologue.

PARTS 2, 3

Vocabulary: Synonyms are words with similar meanings. Draw a line from each word in column A to its synonym in column B. Then use the words in column A to fill in the blanks in the sentences below.

1.	flippant	a.	thoughtful
2.	culminate	b.	disturbance
3.	prolific	c.	disrespectful
4.	agitation	d.	conclude
5.	animosity	e.	culprit
6.	transgressor	f.	enmity
7.	benign	g.	abundant
8.	pensive	h.	good

· ·

1. As the victim of an automobile accident looked over the people on the police lineup, he hoped the _____ would have a guilty expression on his face.

2. Although I was expecting the worst, I had such a(n) _____ visit with my aunt that she invited me back again.

3. My expression changed from _____ to jubilant as I realized the letter from a stranger announced that I had inherited a great deal of money.

4. The tour will _____ in a visit to the Grand Canyon, and then we will return home.

5. Her _____ attitude was inappropriate to the serious circumstances.

6. The artist was so _____ that he ran out of room to store his paintings.

7. The suspect's _____ became obvious when his body trembled as the police questioned him.

8. The _____ between the two neighboring nations finally erupted in warfare.

Parts 2, 3 (cont.)

Questions:

1. How did Hans Hubermann's Christmas gift to Liesel reveal the depth of his feelings for her?

2. How did the Hubermann's financial situation reflect the general state of Germany's economy in the 1930s?

3. Why did Mama Hubermann decide to risk sending Liesel on the important business of laundry pickup and delivery?

4. Why did the Hubermanns avoid any discussion of Liesel's mother in front of her daughter?

5. In what important respect did Hans Junior differ from his father?

6. Why did Hans Junior accuse his father of cowardice? What was the "mistake" Papa Hubermann had committed?

7. Why did the people of Molching hold a bonfire? What shocking realization met Liesel when she listened to the speaker at the bonfire?

8. Why did Papa Hubermann slap Liesel?

9. Why did Papa Hubermann buy a copy of Hitler's *Mein Kampf*?

10. Why did Liesel avoid the mayor's house for some time? And then, why did she change radically and look forward to delivering laundry to the mayor's house?

11. Why did Max Vandenburg read a copy of *Mein Kampf* on the train?

Questions for Discussion:

1. Do you think Liesel deserved to be punished for taking money to mail letters to her mother? Was Rosa justified in meting out such a harsh punishment?

2. Do you think there was some way that Hans could have made peace with his son? Why didn't he?

3. In what ways might Hans Hubermann have been considered a hero and not a coward as he had been accused by his son?

4. What silent understanding do you think passed between Liesel and the mayor's wife? Why do you suppose Ilse Hermann allowed Liesel to browse through her library?

5. Do you think that the thievery practiced by Rudy, Liesel, and the other children was justified?

6. What do you think is the relationship between Max and Hans Hubermann?

7. How is each of Liesel's book titles an ironic comment on the times? What is ironic about the title of Max Vandenburg's book?

Parts 2, 3 (cont.)

Literary Devices:

I. *Symbolism*—A symbol in literature is a person, object, or event that stands for an idea or a set of ideas. What does the book *The Grave Digger's Handbook* symbolize?

_____

_____

What does the conclusion of reading the book symbolize?

_____

_____

II. *Verbal irony*—Verbal irony is a figure of speech in which the speaker says one thing, but intends something quite different. The device of verbal irony may include sarcasm, overstatement, and understatement. For instance, the narrator says that World War II was the result of the Germans' love of burning things. What tells you that this statement should not be taken literally, at face value?

_____

_____

III. *Flashback* and *Flash Forward*—A writer can play with time sequence to achieve particular effects. A flashback is a scene which takes the narrative back to a time before the current point in the plot. A flash forward reveals what will happen at some future point in the story. What instances of flashback and flash forward can you find in this section of *The Book Thief*? What do you learn from these interruptions to the normal sequence of the plot?

_____

_____

_____

IV. *Cliffhanger*—A cliffhanger is a device borrowed from silent serialized films in which an episode would end abruptly at a moment of heightened tension or suspense. In a book it usually appears at the end of a chapter to encourage the reader to continue on in the book. What is the cliffhanger at the end of Part Three?

_____

Writing Activity:

Imagine that you are Hans or Rosa Hubermann and write a journal entry describing your feelings about Liesel and life in Nazi Germany.

PART 4

Vocabulary: Antonyms are words with opposite meanings. Draw a line from each word in column A to its antonym in column B. Then use the words in column A to fill in the blanks in the sentences below.

A	**B**
1. malignant	a. cheerful
2. ostracism	b. confidence
3. capitulate	c. gentle
4. morose	d. benign
5. dormant	e. subtle
6. abrasive	f. acceptance
7. trepidation	g. resist
8. blatant	h. active

. . . .

1. Failure to conform to society's accepted values may lead to a person's _____.

2. In winter, frogs and fish lie underneath the ice in a(n) _____ state.

3. The _____ tone of the speaker angered and offended many in the audience.

4. With great _____, the boy knocked on the door of the spooky old house.

5. "You cannot possibly expect me to believe such a(n) _____ lie!" shouted the angry man.

6. With the enormous loss of troops, the general was forced to _____ to the enemy.

7. It was typical in old silent films for the villain to wear a(n) _____ sneer at all times.

8. Judging from my friend's _____ expression, I assumed he had just received some terrible news.

Part 4 (cont.)

Questions:

1. How did Erik Vandenburg save Hans Hubermann's life in the first World War?

2. How was a relationship forged between Hans Hubermann and Erik Vandenburg's son Max? Why did Hans feel compelled to help Max?

3. Why did Hans's business go into decline after 1933?

4. Why were Max's adolescent peers surprised by his aggressiveness?

5. What burden of guilt did Max Vandenburg bear?

6. Why did Hans risk frightening Liesel terribly?

7. What factors helped to create the bond between Max and Liesel?

Questions for Discussion:

1. What qualities do you think Rosa Hubermann demonstrated after Max's arrival? Were you surprised by her behavior under these challenging circumstances?

2. Do you think Hans and Rosa should have required Max to leave after the hand-holding episode with Liesel?

3. How do you suppose Max's years of street fighting helped him during the years before and during World War II?

4. Do you think Hans was more motivated to help Max for political reasons or his need to keep a promise?

5. Why do you think Max created *The Standover Man* for Liesel? What was significant about the materials he used to make the book?

Literary Devices:

I. *Symbolism*—What do you think the accordion symbolized?

_____

_____

II. *Flashback*—Why do you think the narrator provided a flashback to Hans Hubermann's World War I experiences?

_____

_____

_____

Part 4 (cont.)

III. *Metaphor*—What implied comparison is being made in the following comment about war?

> The conversation of bullets.

_____

_____

IV. *Simile*—A simile is a figure of speech in which two unlike objects are compared using the words "like" or "as." For example:

> Sometimes there was humor in Max Vandenburg's voice, though its physicality was like friction—like a stone being gently rubbed across a large rock.

What is being compared?

_____

Why is this an apt comparison?

_____

_____

Writing Activity:

Return to Max's "Pages from the Basement." Then create your own picture book tribute to a special friend or family member.

PART 5

Vocabulary: Use the words in the Word Box and the clues below to complete the crossword puzzle.

```
WORD BOX
admonish    commence     frugal        malice
amiable     diminutive   hypocrite     rebate
audible     frail        hypothermia   venom
```

Across

1. spending as little as possible

4. able to be heard

5. begin; start

7. extremely small in size

9. return of part of a payment

10. one who practices or professes beliefs that one does not hold

Down

1. physically weak; delicate

2. desire to harm others or see others suffer

3. abnormally low body temperature

4. scold gently

6. good-natured and likeable

8. poison, in a snake or insect

Part 5 (cont.)

Questions:

1. Why did Liesel scavenge from garbage pails on the days she went on her laundry route?

2. How did Max make time pass as he spent days and weeks in the Hubermanns' basement?

3. Why was Liesel outraged against the mayor's wife?

4. Why didn't Rosa Hubermann punish Liesel after learning how Liesel had insulted the mayor's wife?

5. Why had Viktor Chemmel assumed the leadership of the gang of thieves?

6. Why was Tommy Müller punished during the Hitler Youth drill? Why was Rudy Steiner punished along with him?

7. Why did Lisa and Rudy feel compelled to commit a significant robbery by themselves?

8. What evidence showed that almost all of the German population was suffering under the Nazi regime?

Questions for Discussion:

1. Why do you suppose the narrator flashed forward to Rudy Steiner's death? Do you think this knowledge improves or lessens your appreciation of the book?

2. How do you think Max and Liesel felt about one another?

3. In your opinion did Ilse Hermann deserve Liesel's anger?

4. Do you think Rudy deserved the punishment he received at Franz's hands? Could he have avoided it?

5. In what ways did Franz Deutscher embody the attitude of Hitler's regime? How did his surname confirm this?

6. What do you think was significant about the book entitled *The Whistler*? Is there a common theme that connects the books Liesel has stolen?

Literary Devices:

I. *Symbolism*—What did the dream of Max fighting with the *Führer* symbolize?

_____

_____

What did Max's over-written pages of *Mein Kampf* symbolize?

_____

_____

Part 5 (cont.)

II. *Personification*—What is being personified as Liesel thinks about Max while she is visiting the mayor's wife?

> As the book quivered in her [Liesel's] lap, the secret sat in her mouth.
> It made itself comfortable, it crossed its legs.

_____

Why was this better than saying, "Liesel kept her secret about Max to herself"?

_____

_____

Notice how time is personified at the beginning of the chapter titled "The Boxer: End of May." How does Max characterize "time"?

_____

_____

Cooperative Learning Activity: Prediction

Work with a group of your classmates to predict what will happen in the story. Write your predictions in response to each of the following questions:

- Will Rosa and Hans survive the war?
- Will the Nazis capture Max?
- Will Liesel accidentally betray the presence of Max in the Hubermann home?
- Will Rudy turn out to be a heroic figure?
- Will there be serious consequences from Liesel's last encounter with the mayor's wife?

Social Studies Connection: Heroes of World War Two

Do some research to find out about ordinary citizens who risked their lives to hide Jews or help them escape Nazi Germany and the occupied countries. Prepare an oral presentation to deliver to a group of classmates or to the entire class.

Writing Activities:

1. Write about an everyday act of heroism that you have witnessed. What made the actions of the person or people involved heroic?

2. Imagine that you are Rudy Steiner and write a letter to Liesel expressing your true feelings for her. Use episodes from the novel upon which to base your letter.

PART 6

Vocabulary: Word analogies are equations in which the first pair of words has the same relationship as the second set of words. For example: ASCENT is to DESCENT as TRAGEDY is to COMEDY. Both sets of words are opposites. Choose a word from the Word Box to complete each of the analogies below.

> *WORD BOX*
> amble   paradox
> delicate   retreat
> immense   verge
> interior   vigilance

1. ROOF is to EXTERIOR as KITCHEN is to _____.

2. WALK is to _____ as RACE is to SPRINT.

3. STURDY is to MARBLE as _____ is to CRYSTAL.

4. BRINK is to _____ as ATTEMPT is to TRY.

5. BALANCE is to TIGHTROPE WALKER as _____ is to GUARD.

6. _____ is to PUZZLE as FEAR is to TREPIDATION.

7. _____ is to MINUTE as FATIGUED is to RESTED.

8. VICTORIOUS is to ADVANCE as DEFEATED is to _____.

Questions:

1. How did "Death" characterize the year 1942?

2. Why was Christmas Day 1942 a special time for those who resided in Hans Hubermann's home?

3. Why did Max wait so long to reveal his illness to the family?

4. Why did Liesel blame herself for bringing snow into the basement in order to build the snowman?

5. What did Liesel hope to accomplish by bringing presents to the unconscious Max?

6. Why did Rosa Hubermann make an unplanned visit to Liesel's school?

7. Why did Liesel deliberately injure her leg while playing outdoors?

8. Why did Death say that the sky was "the color of Jews"? How did Death respond to the mass destruction of human lives?

Part 6 (cont.)

Questions for Discussion:

1. Why do you think the author has "Death" narrate this tale, using a chatty, somewhat ironic tone? Do you think this adds or detracts from the book's serious themes?

2. Why do you think Rosa Hubermann always wanted to appear tough and unemotional?

3. In what ways did this book offer an unusual characterization of "Death"?

4. Why do you think Liesel was able to enter the mayor's house with ease and rob books each time?

5. How did Liesel's dream about her brother and Max Vandenburg mirror the conflicts in her own life?

Literary Devices:

I. *Simile*—What is being compared in the following passage?

> . . . she [Liesel] stood on Munich Street and watched a single giant cloud come over the hills like a white monster. . . . The sun was eclipsed, and in its place, a white beast with a gray heart watched the town.

_____

_____

Why is this better than saying, "A cloud crossed the sky"?

_____

_____

II. *Cliffhanger*—What is the cliffhanger at the end of page 324?

_____

III. *Symbolism*—What was the symbolic importance of the last book Liesel obtained, *The Dream Carrier*?

_____

_____

_____

Part 6 (cont.)

Social Studies Connections:

1. Do some research to determine why "Death" compared the years 79 and 1346 with the year 1942. What important events happened in these years? What other years might also be used in this comparison?

2. Do some research to learn about the bombing of the city of Cologne in Germany during World War II. How much of the city was destroyed and how many people were killed and wounded?

Writing Activities:

1. Imagine that you are a reporter for a foreign newspaper and interview Max while he is in hiding in the Hubermann's basement. Write some questions you might ask him about his past experiences, current state of mind, and expectations for the future.

2. Imagine that you are the mayor's wife. Write a letter to Liesel explaining the reasons for your actions. In your letter, try to capture the personality and voice of the writer.

PART 7

Vocabulary: Draw a line from each word on the left to its definition on the right. Then use the numbered words to fill in the blanks in the sentences below.

1. depleted   a. fear of future trouble or evil

2. trilogy   b. used up

3. formidable   c. pretend

4. loathsome   d. dreadful; menacing

5. apprehension   e. useless

6. feign   f. unchangeable

7. immutable   g. three-part work of literature

8. futile   h. offensive; disgusting

· ·

1. Having enjoyed the first two plays, I looked forward to seeing the last play in the _____.

2. My feelings of _____ grew as the storm approached.

3. Once our supplies of food and water were _____, we knew we had to be rescued before nightfall.

4. With a cast protecting my broken leg, I knew it would be _____ to try out for the basketball team.

5. Afraid that I would be a(n) _____ competitor, my opponent dropped out of the tennis match.

6. The cause of the _____ odor that filled the kitchen was a glass of milk that had been left out on the counter overnight.

7. Having been tipped off ahead of time, I could only _____ astonishment when everyone cried, "Surprise."

8. Faced with the host's set of _____ rules and regulations, the guests became uncomfortable and left early.

Part 7 (cont.)

Questions:

1. What caused the brief period of contentment for Liesel and Papa Hubermann during the summer of 1942?
2. Why did Rudy want to excel at athletic competition?
3. Why did Liesel conclude that she was a criminal even though Ilse Hermann gave her permission to steal books?
4. Why didn't Death feel sympathy for the Germans who hid in their basements during the air raids?
5. Why did the possible bombing of Molching place Max in particular danger?
6. What service did Liesel perform during the second air raid on Molching?
7. Why did Max have to leave 33 Himmel Street?
8. Why was Hans Hubermann guilt-ridden days after the incident at the march?

Questions for Discussion:

1. Why do you suppose Rudy got himself disqualified from the final race of the day and then left his medals behind?
2. Why do you think the author included entries from the dictionary/thesaurus given Liesel by Ilse Hermann?
3. Why do you think the author placed the parade of Jews on their way to Dachau in the unfolding story of *The Book Thief*?
4. Why might Death have agreed with Hans Hubermann that his act of compassion was "stupid"?

Literary Devices:

I. *Irony*—Why is it ironic that a book helped the Germans live through the second air raid in Molching?

_____

_____

Why is it ironic that Frau Holtzapfels wanted Liesel to continue reading that same book to her?

_____

_____

Why is it ironic that Hans suffered feelings of guilt after giving the dying Jewish man a piece of bread?

_____

Part 7 (cont.)

II. *Allusion*—An allusion is a literary reference to a familiar person, place, or event. Allusions may give readers a common reference point and also confer authenticity on a work of literature. For example, in this section of the novel, the narrator explains that the Jewish prisoners were being marched through the streets of Molching to demonstrate the efficiency of the Dachau work camp. If you are not familiar with the name Dachau, do some research to learn about what happened to prisoners of that camp.

III. *Extended Metaphor*—An extended metaphor is a suggested or implied comparison that continues on. The chapter "The Long Walk to Dachau" begins with the events of the day being compared to "an ocean sky, with whitecap clouds." Scan the chapter and find other examples of events being compared to stormy waters.

_____

_____

_____

IV. *Personification*—What is being personified as Liesel contemplates the glorious summer with Papa that is coming to an abrupt end?

The brightness had shown suffering the way.

_____

_____

Social Studies Connection: Hitler Youth

Do some research to find out how young people were indoctrinated into Nazism. What was the purpose of such organizations? How did they fit into the psychology of fascism and militarism? Prepare a brief written or oral report on your findings.

Writing Activity:

1. Imagine that you are Max and are able to write a letter to the family that has sheltered you before you decided to flee. Express your gratitude to the Hubermanns, your special fondness for Liesel, and your criticism of Nazi Germany as it appeared in Molching.

2. Imagine that you are an objective multi-national observer assigned to report on conditions in Molching during World War II. Write that report.

PART 8

Vocabulary: Use the context to determine the meaning of the underlined word in each of the following sentences. Circle the letter of the word you choose.

1. We asked everyone to wish us good luck before we began our _____ hike up the steep, rocky mountain.

   a. gradual   b. perilous   c. safe   d. fortuitous

2. It is dangerous to return to the fire zone because the ashes are still _____ on the ground.

   a. leaping   b. crackling   c. smoldering   d. dousing

3. I was so absorbed in the book I was reading that I was _____ to the storm that was raging outside my window.

   a. oblivious   b. conscious   c. listening   d. engaging

4. Aware that I had not trained hard enough, I had strong feelings of _____ as I began the race.

   a. anxiety   b. victory   c. exhaustion   d. relief

5. Knowing that I had been out of work for the past year, the doctor agreed to accept _____ payment for the treatment.

   a. anticipated   b. dwindling   c. total   d. partial

6. The rubber patch was only a _____ solution for my tire problem.

   a. permanent   b. temporary   c. practical   d. judicious

7. My students' _____ stares made it perfectly clear that they did not understand the lesson.

   a. accusatory   b. inquisitive   c. vacant   d. disinterested

8. It is _____ to expect an untrained actor to play the part of Hamlet.

   a. dramatic   b. fortunate   c. solemn   d. ludicrous

Questions:

1. Why did "the coat men" visit Alex Steiner's house?
2. Why was Rudy selected for examination by the Nazi medical authorities? What was ironic about his selection?
3. Why were the middle-aged Alex Steiner and Hans Hubermann drafted?
4. How did Hans Hubermann's job in the German army suit him?
5. Why did Liesel and Rudy go to observe the third march of the Jews to Dachau?
6. Why did Liesel take Rudy to his father's abandoned shop on Christmas night?

Part 8 (cont.)

Questions for Discussion:

1. What do you suppose transformed Rudy Steiner from an apple thief into a bread giver?

2. Why do you think Hans Hubermann's letters home were so brief?

3. Why do you think the author showed German soldiers, such as Hans Hubermann, performing civilian tasks instead of being shown on a battlefield? And why did he focus on ordinary German civilians during wartime?

4. What do you think Max's book revealed about the power of words? How might words represent both beauty and evil? What message do you think the story imparted?

5. Why do you think Liesel did not seize the opportunity to kiss Rudy inside his father's shop on Christmas night?

Literary Devices:

I. *Personification*—What is being personified in the following passage?

> Even when they made it around the corner, away from the center
> of the wreckage, the haze of the collapsed building attempted to
> follow. It was white and warm, and it crept behind them.

Why is it better than saying, "smoke from the collapsed buildings filled the air"?

II. *Allegory*—An allegory is a work in which characters, events, or settings symbolize, or represent, something else. Max Vandenburg's illustrated story for Liesel is allegorical because the events and actions are symbolic and not intended to be taken literally. For instance:

> Soon, the demand for the lovely ugly words and symbols increased
> to such a point that the forests grew. Many people were needed to
> maintain them. Some were employed to climb the trees and throw the
> words down to those below. They were then fed directly into the remainder
> of the Fuhrer's people, not to mention those who came back for more.

How do the words and symbols that sprout from these trees relate to the political situation in Hitler's Germany?

III. *Symbolism*—What did Rudy's lined-up dominoes, described at the beginning of Part 8, symbolize?

Writing Activity:

Write a paragraph in which you consider the saying "No good deed goes unpunished." How does this saying relate to this section of The Book Thief?

PART 9

Vocabulary: Use the context to figure out the meaning of the underlined word in each of the following sentences. Then compare your answer with a dictionary definition.

1. It was difficult to keep the present a surprise because it <u>protruded</u> from his front pocket.

   Your definition _____

   Dictionary definition _____

2. To those who have never suffered from poison ivy, the bright green three-leaved plant seems <u>innocuous</u> enough.

   Your definition _____

   Dictionary definition _____

3. Even if you are in a terrible mood, please attempt a <u>semblance</u> of civility.

   Your definition _____

   Dictionary definition _____

4. The angry parent delivered a <u>reprimand</u> to her son who had worried her by staying out well past his curfew.

   Your definition _____

   Dictionary definition _____

5. The engineer will blow the whistle three <u>consecutive</u> times as the train approaches the station.

   Your definition _____

   Dictionary definition _____

Questions:

1. How did Ilse Hermann prepare for Liesel's next visit?

2. What disturbing news did Michael Holtzapfel bring to Himmel Street? Why did this news devastate Rosa Hubermann as well as his own mother?

3. What finally laid the ghost of Liesel's brother to rest?

4. Why did Hans Hubermann change seats on the military vehicle?

5. Why was Hans Hubermann allowed to return home?

Part 9 (cont.)

Questions for Discussion:

1. Do you think Ilse Hermann was a Nazi sympathizer?
2. Why do you suppose Liesel didn't discuss the mayor's wife with Rudy?
3. Why do you think the author evoked sympathy for wounded German soldiers?
4. Why do you think Michael Holtzapfel killed himself?
5. Why do you think Rudy's attitude toward thievery changed?
6. What did Death mean when he commented about Liesel as she observed the dying survivor of the plane crash, "She did not back away or try to fight me, but I know that something told the girl I was there . . . she knew me and she looked me in my face and she did not look away . . . we both moved on"?
7. Do you think that Rudy and Liesel tried to aid the downed "enemy" pilot?

Social Studies Connection:

Do some research to learn about the siege of Leningrad during World War II. Discover why the siege had a devastating effect upon the German civilian population.

Literary Devices:

I. *Metaphor*—What is being compared in the following passages that described Michael Hotzapfel's wound?

> A bandaged hand fell out of his coat sleeve and cherries of blood were seeping through the wrapping . . . the cherries of blood had grown into plums.

Why is it better than just saying that "his hand bled"?

II. *Irony*—What was ironic about the death of Reinhold Zucker?

Literary Element: Characterization

How would you characterize Death as he appears in this novel? Select five adjectives that epitomize this character and give an example of his commentary that illustrates each character trait.

Writing Activity

Use the elements of character that you selected in the prior activity to write a character sketch of Death as he appears in this novel.

PART 10, EPILOGUE

Vocabulary: Draw a line from each word on the left to its meaning on the right. Then use the numbered words to answer each of the questions below.

1.	overcast		a.	free from error
2.	unkempt		b.	person or persons saddened by death of a loved one
3.	threshold		c.	determine by reasoning
4.	pensive		d.	overspread or covered with clouds
5.	accurate		e.	expressing thoughtfulness, usually marked by sadness
6.	bereaved		f.	firmly resolved or determined
7.	calculate		g.	place of entering or beginning
8.	resolute		h.	untidy; messy

. . . .

1. If you observe that the sky is *overcast*, what items might you carry when you leave the house?

    _____

2. How might someone improve his *unkempt* appearance?

    _____

3. What worries might you have on the *threshold* of a new career?

    _____

4. Under what circumstances might someone seem *pensive*?

    _____

5. If you want your bookkeeping to be absolutely *accurate*, what steps might you take?

    _____

6. In your culture, how do the *bereaved* behave and dress?

    _____

7. How might someone *calculate* the time it would take to travel to their destination during rush hour?

    _____

8. Under what circumstances have you needed to be *resolute*?

    _____

Part 10, Epilogue (cont.)

Questions:

1. How did Liesel survive the air strike on Himmel Street? How did words once again save her life?
2. Why did Liesel attend each time Jews were marched through Molching?
3. How did Rudy save Liesel's life?
4. How did Ilse Hermann inspire Liesel to write her own story?
5. What did Liesel realize when she found Rudy's body after the bombing? How did she attempt to reach him?
6. Who took care of Liesel after she was orphaned for the second time?
7. Who was the unexpected survivor of the war?

Questions for Discussion:

1. How did the author show the random quality of death during war time?
2. Do you think those who observed Liesel's whipping at the hands of the German soldiers should have offered their help?
3. Why do you think Liesel destroyed the book in Ilse Hermann's library?
4. Toward the end of the book, how had Liesel developed a love-hate relationship with words?
5. Whose death had the greatest effect upon you?
6. What were the qualities that Hans Hubermann possessed that made Death consider him one of the best of men?
7. Why do you suppose the narrator did not reveal what happened to Liesel in the years between her reunion with Max and the time of her death?

Literary Devices:

I. *Metaphor*—What two comparisons are being made in the following passage:

> . . . I looked up and saw the tin-can planes. I watched their stomachs open and the bombs drop casually out.

_____

_____

Why are these apt comparisons?

_____

_____

Part 10, Epilogue (cont.)

II. *Dramatic Irony*—Dramatic irony, used more often in plays than in prose fiction, refers to a situation in which the audience or the reader is aware of something that a character does not know. Why is the first short, poetic episode about Michael Holtzapfel an example of dramatic irony? Who was unaware of the event at this point?

_____

_____

_____

III. *Symbolism*—What Christian symbolism surrounded the figure of Max? In what ways was Max a Christ-like figure?

_____

_____

_____

_____

Literary Element: Narrative Technique

There are various ways of manipulating time sequence when telling a story. Consider how flashback and flash forward have been used throughout the novel. In this section, the narrative shifts rapidly between past, present, and future. What effect does this have on the story?

Writing Activity:

Write the first three pages of a book about your life. Compose on the computer or in long-hand, but write quickly and do not edit until you finish the pages.

CLOZE ACTIVITY

The following passage has been taken from Part 10. Read it through completely. Then fill in each blank with a word that makes sense. Afterwards, you may compare your language with that of the author.

       She [Liesel] had seen her brother die with one eye open, one still in a dream. She had said goodbye to her _____[1] and imagined her lonely wait for a _____[2] back home to oblivion. A woman of _____[3] had laid herself down, her scream traveling _____[4] street, till it fell sideways like a _____[5] coin starved of momentum. A young man _____[6] hung by a rope made of Stalingrad _____.[7] She had watched a bomber pilot die _____[8] a metal case. She had seen a _____[9] man who had twice given her the _____[10] beautiful pages of her life marched to _____[11] concentration camp. And at the center of _____[12] of it, she saw the *Führer* shouting _____[13] words and passing them around.

       Those images _____[14] the world, and it stewed in her _____[15] she sat with the lovely books and _____[16] manicured titles. It brewed in her as _____[17] eyed the pages full to the brims _____[18] their bellies with paragraphs and words.

       You _____,[19] she thought.

       You lovely bastards.

       Don't make _____[20] happy. Please, don't fill me up and _____[21] me think that something good can come _____[22] any of this. Look at my bruises. _____[23] at this graze. Do you see the _____[24] inside me? Do you see it growing _____[25] your very eyes, eroding me? I don't _____[26] to hope for anything anymore. I don't _____[27] to pray that Max is alive and _____.[28] Or Alex Steiner.

       Because the world does not _____[29] them.

She tore a page from the _____[30] and ripped it in half.

       Then a _____.[31]

       Soon, there was nothing but scraps of _____[32] littered between her legs and all around _____.[33] The words. Why did they have to _____?[34] Without them, there wouldn't be any of _____.[35] Without words, the *Führer* was nothing. There _____[36] be no limping prisoners, no need for _____[37] or worldly tricks to make us feel _____.[38]

       What good were the words?

POST-READING ACTIVITIES AND DISCUSSION QUESTIONS

1. Return to the K-W-L chart on the Holocaust that you began in the Pre-Reading Activities on page six of this study guide. Correct any errors that you may have made in column one and record what you have learned in column three. Compare your responses to those of others who have read the same book.

2. Why do you think the novel was titled *The Book Thief*? Why did Liesel steal books? Was she a thief? What did the books mean to her? If you had to choose a different title for the novel, what would it be?

3. Return to the Venn diagram that you began on page eleven of this study guide. Add further information about Liesel and Rudy. Discuss your entries with others who have read *The Book Thief*. Did all the readers form the same impressions of those two characters? What character traits did Liesel and Rudy have in common?

4. Review the titles of the books Liesel finds or steals. What is significant about each title? How does each reflect on the personal situations of the characters and on the larger political situation of Germany during the war?

5. Why did the author choose "Death" as the narrator of the story? How was death characterized? How did this characterization reflect upon the nature of Life? How was this characterization of death different from others in literature and art?

6. **Art Connection:** Create an illustrated book, as Max did, that tells in simple language and line drawings about someone you admire. Unlike Max who wrote over *Mein Kampf*, you may relate your story to another work of literature that is significant to your character.

7. Write a sequel telling what happens to Liesel in the years between her reunion with Max and her death many years later. Imagine what might have happened to Liesel during this long period of time.

8. Scan the short pieces of free verse that are scattered throughout the book. What purpose do they serve? Choose one piece to discuss its meaning and purpose in the story.

9. **Social Studies Connection:** Do some research on the economic and social conditions of Germany during World War II. What factors contributed to this situation? How did Germany eventually manage to recover after the war?

10. **Symbolism:** Trace the symbol of the accordion throughout the book. Under what circumstances did Hans acquire the accordion? How did he use it during his lifetime? How did it survive his death?

Post-Reading Activities and Discussion Questions (cont.)

11. **Literary Element: Theme**
    A theme in a literary work is a controlling idea or message. *The Book Thief* has several important themes. Consider the following themes and discuss how each is developed in the novel:
    - individual identity *vs.* conformity to social expectations
    - coming to terms with abandonment and loss
    - overcoming stereotypes
    - concern with self *versus* concern for others
    - the power of words
    - the human need for self-expression
    - forming ties with others

12. **Social Studies Connection:** Do some research to learn about the purpose and organization of concentration camps in Germany and Eastern Europe. How did this system fit in with Hitler's Final Solution?

13. Why do you think the author had you witness the Holocaust through the eyes of ordinary German citizens? Why were there no heroes or villains, except for Hitler, portrayed in the book?

14. **Literature Circle:** Have a literature circle discussion in which you tell your personal reactions to *The Book Thief*. Here are some questions to help your literature circle begin a discussion.
    - Do you identify with Liesel in any way? Do you identify with any other character?
    - Did this book provide you with any new insights into the lives of people you would never have known otherwise?
    - Do you think the characters and the way they spoke were presented in a realistic fashion? Why or why not?
    - Which character did you admire the most? The least?
    - Who else would you like to read this novel? Why?
    - If you could have a discussion with Markus Zusak, the author of this book, what would you ask him?
    - If you were to choose one moment in the book that you found most moving, what would it be?

SUGGESTIONS FOR FURTHER READING

Fiction

* Boyne, John. *The Boy in the Striped Pajamas*. David Fickling Books.
  Broner, Peter. *Night of the Broken Glass*. Station Hill Press, Inc.
* Greene, Bette. *Summer of My German Soldier*. Puffin.
* Kerr, M.E. *Gentlehands*. HarperCollins.
  Levitin, Sonia. *The Return*. Fawcett.
  Moran, Thomas. *The Man in the Box*. CreateSpace.
* Orlev, Uri. *The Island on Bird Street*. HMH Books.
  _____. *The Man from the Other Side*. Puffin.
  _____. *Run, Boy, Run!* Puffin.
  Pausewang, Gudrun. *The Final Journey*. Puffin.
  Schmidt, Gary. *Mara's Stories: Glimmers in the Darkness*. Square Fish.
  Shreve, Anita. *Resistance*. Back Bay Books.
* Spinelli, Jerry. *Milkweed*. Random House.
* Yolen, Jane. *The Devil's Arithmetic*. Puffin.

Nonfiction

Bitton-Jackson, Livia. *I Have Lived a Thousand Years: Growing Up in the Holocaust*. Simon Pulse.
Boas, Jacob. *We Are Witnesses: Five Diaries of Teens Who Died in the Holocaust*. Square Fish.
* Frank, Anne. *Anne Frank: Diary of a Young Girl*. Bantam.
  Gruener, Ruth. *Destined to Live*. Scholastic.
  Langer, Lawrence, C. ed. *Art From the Ashes*. Oxford University Press.
  Lobel, Anita. *No Pretty Pictures: A Child of War*. Green Willow.
  Opdyke, Irene. *In My Hands: Memoirs of a Holocaust Rescuer*. Laurel Leaf.
  Rossel, Seymour. *The Holocaust: The World and the Jews, 1933–1945*. Behrman House, Inc.
* Wiesel, Eli. *Night*. Hill and Wang.

Some Other Books by Markus Zusak

Fighting Ruben Wolfe. Scholastic.
I Am the Messenger. Knopf.
Underdogs. Arthur A. Levine Books.

* NOVEL-TIES Study Guides are available for these titles.

ANSWER KEY

Prologue, Part 1

Vocabulary: 1. j 2. f 3. a 4. b 5. c 6. i 7. h 8. e 9. d 10. g; 1. vehement 2. auspicious 3. morbidity 4. abducted 5. frigid 6. raucous 7. lethal 8. berate 9. catalyst 10. affable

Questions: 1. Death found the sorrow of the survivors painful. 2. Death made the mistake of lingering near the train line and becoming curious about Liesel, the girl near the tracks. 3. While aboard the train, Liesel's younger brother died. 4. The children were supposed to be placed in foster care in January 1939 because their mother was too ill and poor to care for them properly. As a family in which the father was a communist, they had been persecuted in Nazi Germany. 5. Death thought it was futile for the poor to travel to escape poverty because they would inevitably find a new version of their problem when they reached their destination. 6. The book about grave digging became significant to Liesel because she found it on the day when she last saw her brother and mother. 7. Liesel adjusted to her new foster home because of the patience, kindness, and sensitivity of her foster father, Hans Hubermann. 8. Having never had the opportunity to go to school, Liesel entered school in Munich as an illiterate. When she was placed in a class with young children who were just learning the alphabet, she was humiliated. 9. Rudy's father was trying to teach his son that it was unsafe to do anything that might mock or openly criticize Nazi policy, such as doing something that could be construed as admiration for Jesse Owens. 10. Liesel insisted on participating in the reading examination because her reading practice with Papa Hubermann had made her confident in her ability to read. When she stood before the class however, Liesel froze when it became clear to her that the text was beyond her ability. In a last attempt to save face, she recited a memorized part of *The Gravedigger's Handbook*, causing her classmates to laugh at her. 11. In September 1939, Germany invaded Poland, sparking World War II and an increase in the number of deaths worldwide.

Parts 2, 3

Vocabulary: 1. c 2. d 3. g 4. b 5. f 6. e 7. h 8. a; 1. transgressor 2. benign 3. pensive 4. culminate 5. flippant 6. prolific 7. agitation 8. animosity

Questions: 1. The fact that Hans had sacrificed sixteen of his precious hand-rolled cigarettes to trade for two books for Liesel, revealed that he understood her passion for books and loved her sufficiently to give up his only luxury for her sake. 2. The difficult financial situation of the Hubermanns and their neighbors indicated that Germany's economy in the 1930s was weak, and that there was much hardship in the nation. 3. Mama Hubermann decided to risk sending Liesel on the important business of laundry pickup and delivery because she was losing customers during the hard times, and hoped that people would pity Liesel enough to continue to employ her foster mother. 4. The Hubermanns avoided any discussion of Liesel's mother in front of her daughter because they assumed the woman had met with a terrible fate at the hands of the Nazis. 5. Hans Junior, unlike his warm and sensitive father, was cold, cruel, and unswerving in his devotion to Hitler. 6. Hans Junior accused his father of cowardice because he had not joined the Nazi Party; the "mistake" Papa Hubermann had committed was to have painted over the slurs evildoers had scrawled on the outside of Jewish shops and homes. 7. The people of Molching held a bonfire to purge their community of all the "defeatist" literature and objects that predated Hitler and Nazism. When Liesel heard the speaker at the bonfire, she came to realize that her own parents had been persecuted because they were Communists. 8. Papa Hubermann slapped Liesel because he wanted to impress upon her the dire necessity of pretending allegiance to Hitler; otherwise, she would be persecuted and perhaps even killed by Nazi thugs. 9. Papa Hubermann bought a copy of Hitler's *Mein Kampf* in order to pretend allegiance to the Nazi Party, which would not formally accept him in any case. 10. For some time, Liesel avoided the mayor's house for fear that the mayor's wife, who had seen her steal a book from the bonfire, would denounce her; then, her feelings changed radically, and she looked forward to delivering the laundry once the mayor's wife let her spend time in her library handling and reading the books. 11. Max Vandenburg read a copy of *Mein Kampf* on the train in order to establish his Aryan credentials and hide his Jewish background.

Part 4

Vocabulary: 1. d 2. f 3. g 4. a 5. h 6. c 7. b 8. e; 1. ostracism 2. dormant 3. abrasive 4. trepidation 5. blatant 6. capitulate 7. malignant 8. morose

Questions: 1. Erik Vandenburg saved Hans Hubermann's life by volunteering him for a menial duty on the day of a battle while the rest of the men went into battle; only Hubermann survived on that day. 2. Once World War I ended, Hans contacted Erik's family to express his gratitude to the man who saved his life and try to return his accordion. Erik's widow refused to take back the instrument, but acknowledged Hans's offer of help in the future. Max, as a very young boy, was present at that meeting. Years later, Hans felt compelled to help Max because he'd promised Max's mother to help her after the death of Erik Vandenburg. 3. Because Hans had painted over the Jewish slur on Kleinmann's door and then had hesitated to join the Nazi Party, he began to lose the business of staunch Nazi sympathizers and those who feared to show a lack of sympathy by patronizing dissidents. 4. Max's peers were surprised by his aggressiveness because they accepted the stereotype of Jews, one that characterized them as passively accepting violence aimed at them. 5. Max Vandenburg bore the burden of survivor's guilt: he had allowed himself to be saved by his old friend and boxing opponent, Walter Kugler, and had walked away from his doomed family without looking back. 6. Hans risked frightening Liesel terribly in order to compel her to remain silent about the Jewish man hidden in the basement; a word to anyone would have had dire consequences for the family. 7. A bond between Max and Liesel developed because they both had nightmares about abandonment, had been forced to turn outside their own families for help, experienced survivor's guilt, and had a love of reading.

Part 5

Vocabulary: Across—1. frugal 4. audible 5. commence 7. diminutive 9. rebate 10. hypocrite; Down—1. frail 2. malice 3. hypothermia 4. admonish 6. amiable 8. venom

Questions: 1. Liesel scavenged newspapers from garbage pails because she knew that the pages of text and crossword puzzles would be a welcomed gift for Max. 2. To make time pass, Max read the newspapers and did the crossword puzzles that Liesel brought him, did exercises, and prepared pages of *Mein Kampf* to be revised as his own memoir. 3. Liesel was outraged against the mayor's wife because the loss of their business spelled increased poverty for her foster family; also, she would now be cut off from the library; and most of all, because she sensed the hypocrisy behind the mayor's stated decision to sacrifice common comforts as part of the war effort. 4. Rosa Hubermann did not punish Liesel after learning how Liesel had insulted the mayor's wife because, even if she believed any of this story, she realized that nothing she or Liesel had done could have changed the situation. 5. Viktor Chemmel, and not any of the former members, had assumed the leadership because there was no one else in the gang of thieves who could steal without impunity and could direct the others to steal. 6. Tommy Müller was punished during the Hitler Youth drill because he was too deaf to respond to the order to halt marching. Rudy Steiner was punished along with him for daring to defend his friend. 7. Rudy felt compelled to commit a robbery to avenge the series of insults he had suffered at the hands of the Nazi youth and the gang of thieves; and Liesel needed to seek further revenge against the mayor's wife and steal back the book *The Whistler*. 8. Three things make it clear that almost all of the German population, not just the Jews, were suffering economically: Rudy Steiner starving, Liesel's family losing most of their sources of income and feeling hunger, and people standing in line just to buy a potato.

Part 6

Vocabulary: 1. interior 2. amble 3. delicate 4. verge 5. vigilance 6. paradox 7. immense 8. retreat

Questions: 1. "Death" characterized the year 1942 as a time of inordinate suffering and too many deaths. 2. Although there were no presents or festive foods, the residents of Hans Hubermann's house were in good spirits on Christmas Day when Liesel brought snow into Max's basement. They played, built a snowman and temporarily forgot their problems. 3. Max waited a long time to reveal his illness to the family because he did not want to cause them additional inconvenience or pose a greater threat to their security. 4. Liesel blamed herself for bringing snow into the basement in order to build the snowman because she feared that the increased cold had made Max ill. 5. Liesel hoped that by bringing presents to the unconscious Max she would somehow restore him to health. 6. Rosa made an unplanned visit to Liesel's school in order to inform Liesel that Max had awakened from his coma under the guise of scolding her for losing a hairbrush. 7. Liesel deliberately injured her leg while playing outdoors in order to get Papa Hubermann outside to attend her, where she could whisper to him that their basement was about to be inspected by Nazi officials. 8. Death said that the sky was "the color of Jews" because with the constant operation of the gas chambers and crematoria, the remains of the Jewish people were released into the atmosphere; Death responded to the mass destruction of human lives with compassion and disbelief.

Part 7

Vocabulary: 1. b 2. g 3. d 4. h 5. a 6. c 7. f 8. e; 1. trilogy 2. apprehension 3. depleted 4. futile 5. formidable 6. loathsome 7. feign 8. immutable

Questions: 1. The cause of the brief period of contentment for Liesel and Papa Hubermann during the summer of 1942 was the increased employment of Papa as people needed their blinds painted black for the coming air raids. During this time, the two shared work, music, and much enjoyable companionship. 2. It was important to Rudy to excel at athletic competition because he wanted to prove to Franz Deustcher and his gang of brutes in the Hitler Youth that he was a superb athlete; he also wanted to impress Liesel. 3. Even though Ilse Hermann in her letter to Liesel forgave her for taking books from her library, Liesel felt like a criminal for avoiding a meeting with the woman who was so kind to her. 4. Death did not feel sympathy for the Germans who hid in their basements during the air raids because they were to some extent complicit in the Nazi atrocities and because they had at least the chance of escape and freedom, unlike those in the concentration camps. 5. The possible bombing of Molching placed Max in particular danger because as a Jew in hiding, he could not enter a safe shelter. 6. During the second air raid on Molching, Liesel was able to quell the fear of her foster mother and their neighbors by reading aloud from *The Whistler*, one of her treasured stolen books. 7. Max had to leave 33 Himmel Street after Hans Hubermann's act of compassion to the Jewish prisoner on parade placed Max in jeopardy from a likely house search. 8. Hans was guilt-ridden because the Gestapo never came for him, making Max's departure an unnecessary act.

Part 8
Vocabulary: 1. b 2. c 3. a 4. a 5. d 6. b 7. c 8. d
Questions: 1. The "coat men" came to Alex Steiner's house to recruit Rudy (who had shown extraordinary athletic prowess) to their elite school for Nazi youth. 2. Rudy was selected for examination by the Nazi medical authorities because of his academic standing and because of the physical prowess he had demonstrated during the athletic competition. It was ironic that Rudy was selected because he hated the Nazis and he didn't want to join their upper echelons as an officer. 3. The middle-aged Alex Steiner and Hans Hubermann were drafted as a punishment for non-cooperation with the Nazi regime: Steiner had refused to let his son go to officer's training camp, and Hubermann had been vilified for helping a Jew in need during the Dachau work camp parade. 4. Hans Hubermann's job during the war, to clean up after air raid strikes, suited him because it called upon his resourceful and compassionate nature as he repaired damaged buildings and aided survivors of the air strikes. 5. Liesel attended the march, hoping to catch sight of Max; Rudy attended because he wanted to distribute bread to the starving walkers. 6. Liesel took Rudy to his father's shop in order to "steal" a Christmas present for him, as an act of both kindness and defiance.

Part 9
Vocabulary: 1. protruded–stuck out or projected 2. innocuous–harmless; innocent 3. semblance–outward show or appearance 4. reprimand–reproof; scolding 5. consecutive–following one after the other
Questions: 1. Ilse Hermann prepared for Liesel's next visit to her library by leaving out a plate of cookies, by leaving out a book she had selected, and by greeting Liesel when she appeared. 2. Michael Holtzapfel brought the news that his brother had been killed; Rosa Hubermann was also devastated because from Michael she learned that her own son was in Stalingrad, where the fighting was intense and the death toll was enormous. 3. The ghost of Liesel's brother was finally laid to rest when Liesel expressed gratitude to the mayor's wife, which showed her growing ability to love and forgive. 4. Hans Hubermann changed his seat from the back of the military vehicle to a seat in the middle in response to Reinhold Zucker's bullying. 5. Hans Hubermann was allowed to return home for a few weeks while his injured leg healed. Afterwards he would return to an army desk job.

Part 10, Epilogue
Vocabulary: 1. d 2. h 3. g 4. e 5. a 6. b 7. c 8. f; Answers to the questions will vary.
Questions: 1. The Hubermanns, along with the Steiners and some of their other neighbors, were killed in a surprise air strike; Liesel didn't die along with them because she was down in the cellar at the time reading the book Max had created for her. In a sense, therefore, the words in the book saved her life. 2. Liesel attended each time Jews were marched through Molching because she hoped to catch sight of Max and be able to offer him help. 3. Rudy saved Liesel's life by pulling her off the road after the whipping she received for running to Max during the work parade. 4. Ilse Hermann inspired Liesel to write her own story by giving her a blank journal to write in and encouraging her to use her gift of expression. 5. When Liesel found Rudy's body after the bombing, she realized that she had always loved him. She attempted to reach him by giving him the kiss he had always asked for. 6. Ilse Hermann took care of Liesel after she was orphaned for the second time. 7. Max Vandenburg, concentration camp victim, was the unexpected survivor of the war.